The Kitty, the Wind and the Magic Umbrella

A STORY ABOUT WHAT CAN GO WRONG WHEN YOU ARE DISOBEDIENT

Cora Butler-Jones, PhD

Chery Hardi: Contributing Illustrator

WORKBOOK PRESS LLC
187 E Warm Springs Rd,
Suite B285, Las Vegas, NV 89119, USA

Website: https://workbookpress.com/
Hotline: 1-888-818-4856
Email: admin@workbookpress.com

Ordering Information:
Quantity sales. Special discounts are available on quantity purchases by corporations, associations, and others.
For details, contact the publisher at the address above.

ISBN-13:   978-1-956876-28-4 (Paperback Version)
                    978-1-956876-29-1 (Digital Version)

REV. DATE: 10/11/2021

This book is dedicated to Xairis; Athena, Elisabeth's new baby Apollo, and Anthony's boys. This is for the next generation of obedient children!

Introduction

This story is written to help children learn the value of obedience. What happens when you are told to go to bed on time, never to go out in the night without adult supervision, to always ask for help from adults when you are in trouble, these children did not listen. In this story, Kitty had an adventure that tested the children's determination to be good.

It is easy to disobey rules but much harder to face the consequences after doing so as it is not easy to say you are sorry for something you were told not to do.

Luckily in this story, there is an umbrella that the children's parents bought in an antique shop in London that they found just before they went out into the night.

The umbrella is a metaphor and represents the need for the constant presence of an adult for protection.

Hi, my name is Kate, and my little brother is Aiden. On Christmas, we found a black kitty in our home under our tree, and from that time on this wonderful curious kitty was always with me. The kitty was happy, deeply grateful, and connected to our family, who took her in and out of the snow after being properly delivered to us on Christmas day with the fireplace a glow. We kept her clean, gave her lots of yummy food to make her feel welcome we adorned her with a big red bow.

But then the winter wind was swirling outdoors, you see. Mr. Winter seemed angry for some reason, and I thought, *was he angry at me?* Mr. Winter was becoming well-known during this post Christmas winter season. Many people were complaining about being cold right down to their bones.

We sought the owner of Kitty. We sent out lost kitty claims, yet at the same time, we were all deciding her name. The knowledge that a previous owner could come to get her any day now did not lessen our care or determination. It seemed we thought she was at least unaware! It was our family's goal to make her feel welcome and keep her out of the cold and in our family until we grew old.

That night, as we lay asleep in our beds, we suddenly heard a *pop, pop, pop* over our heads. My brother, Kitty, and I thought we heard firecrackers or gunshots. Slowly we awakened and slid across the gleaming wood floor, then off to the window to see if there could be more.

Pop! Pop! Pop!

We heard the sound again as we tiptoed across the room, frightened of what we soon would behold, perhaps a creature from space.

Pop! Pop! Pop!

We made haste and made it to the window. We looked at each other in fear, and then we slowly eased upward to see if the space monsters were near.

As we looked out our window with the kitty beside us, we realized it was worse than we thought. The trees were coming to life, pulling up their roots and unfurling their gigantic branch hands. The halo of branches looked like hair all covered in ice. As they moved in the moonlight as if to a dance, some stumbled and fell and snapped into pieces, making a loud thud.

We all watched in a trance. Initially we thought they were attacking. How could we know with all that cracking? *Crack!* Wow, what a loud sound. Ice was all over the trees, and they seemed angry.

Snap! Snap! Snap!

As we leaned close to the window and tried to make out a black blur, we realized it was our kitty cat! She was out there among the trees, causing them to dodge her. Ice was forming all over her black fur. She was running with haste, just as fast as she could toward our big red barn. We watched in horror, and we were frozen in place, right where we stood.

Pop, pop, pop!

We came out of our trance and realized that what we saw was not really a tree dance. We were fearful and frozen to the window. And after what seemed like an eternity, it happened. The trees began to fall one by one. Pieces of them crashed down, falling on our shed and cars outside.

There goes Miss Kitty, once again wandering off on her own, just as if she never found a home.

We were gripped with fear but determined not to cry. Our parents seemed locked in a deep sleep. We could not awaken them, nor could the storm with the rain, ice, and wind.

Our beloved Kitty was out in the stormy moonlit night, so we thought we follow her like sheep! After all, surely it was safer inside. We had an obligation to care for our new sweet Kitty. We couldn't stay in our house and hide, right? So we crept down the stairs, past an ocean of darkness, thinking, *Shouldn't the front door be closer than this?*

After what seemed like an eternity, we made it to the closet door. Then we realized it was cold inside, especially on the floor. We looked at each other. We whispered in low tones.

Then my brother started to shiver and whispered in a cloud of cold breath, "I am cold to my bones. We are going to freeze to death!"

We wondered why it was so cold inside. There was no night-light to guide through the house. And where was the heat? What was that rustle? Was that a mouse?

Mom and Dad were in a deep sleep. The fire was roaring in their room, so toasty and sweet. They never heard us get up, or even the noisy stairs as they creaked!

Creak, creak, creak! We made it to the closet door. We never stopped to think of the danger that could befall us by going after our new kitty and saving her with no permission. But it was a must! We looked for a flashlight and other items of outer clothing for bad weather in our closet. I found a beautiful unusual-looking umbrella way in the dark corner of the closet.

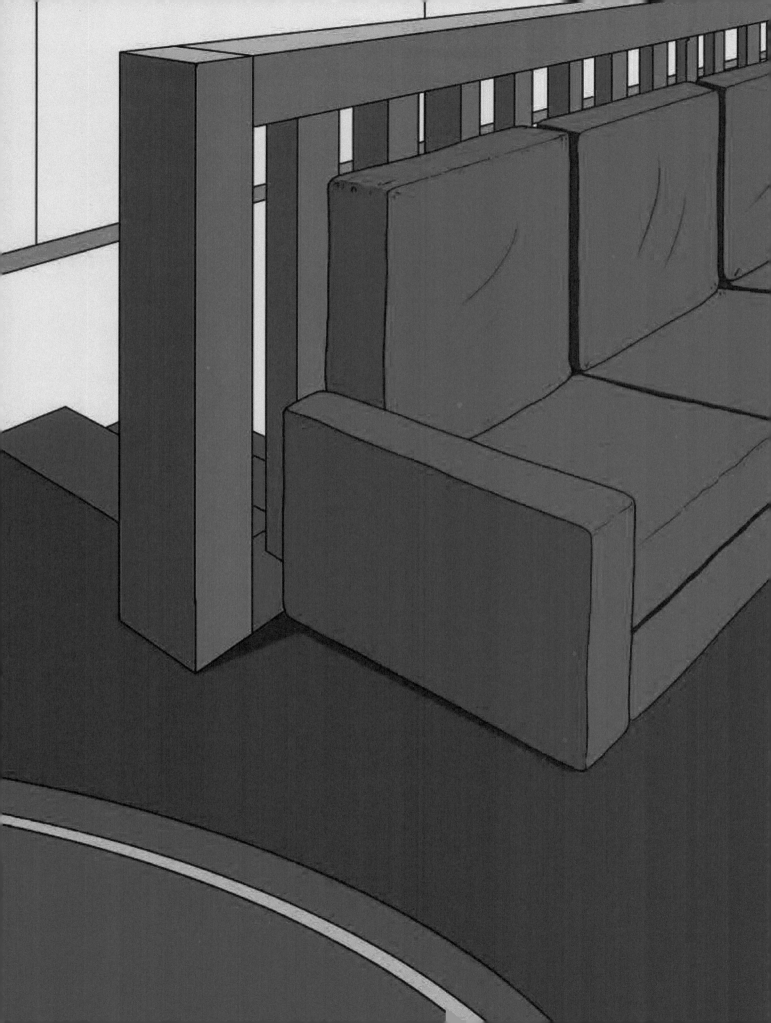

We grabbed the flashlight from its designated space. It was there like always, like an old friend. It made us feel safe. It was in the same spot every day in case of a blackout. We also took the umbrella, a splendid large royal blue it was. Mom brought it back from England. Mom said something about being expensive and from a designer's best in England. It could handle any storm. It was rather large. Mom said it is especially made with a magic handle that was wooden and hand carved.

Pop! Pop! Pop!

We knew we had better hurry. I could hear myself talking inside my head. My inner voice was saying, *No, no, no, Mom wouldn't like this idea at all.* I then went on to get our bright-yellow raincoats with its matching hats and red boots and helped my brother put his rain gear on because he was still small. You see, we are only eight and five. Of course, I am older. I am smarter than him, and I am a lot more bolder! I would protect him and Kitty.

I know, I will use my umbrella to protect us. It will be a piece of cake, I thought. *So why am I shivering? Am I nervous that we could get caught?*

I finally completed the task of getting both of us dressed for outdoors, and off we went to rescue Kitty and get her out of this mess! Now to unlock the mystery of that umbrella, which I had hoped would keep us dry. I was so scared. *Now am I going to cry?*

So we were now downstairs in the hall, opening the door.

Then *crash, bang, pop!* The largest tree branch ever known fell through the roof on the hall floor. The gusts of wind were so strong they opened the front door. My magic umbrella was slightly open, and the gust of wind opened it all the way.

And then we were suddenly flying out through our wrought iron gate, holding the umbrella and clutching each other. Our eyes were opened wide, mouths opened wider, screaming. But it was too late.

We were flying up, up, up into the wind like a kite or a paper airplane glider.

Pop! Pop! Pop!

The noise was now clear to see from our vantage point. It was quite an amazing sight. The day was now lighter. The ice was well-formed. The rain had all but stopped. We were twirling in the air, caught in the wind like a top. Then we spotted our kitty walking across the acres toward the big red barn.

We shouted, "Look out, Kitty."

We struggled to stay calm. My brother seemed frightened beyond belief that he couldn't do much more than utter a tiny shriek.

Finally, the wind gently set us down. Unfortunately for us, we were set down in the middle of our pond. The pond was frozen, or so we thought. As we walked across it, there was a loud sound.

Crackle! Pop! Pop! Pop! Pop! Pop!

A tree fell and whacked the pond. We stood in horror as we saw a large crack that revealed icy water that was slowly creeping across the ice.

Pop, pop, pop!

Oh no, we thought. *We're goners for sure.*

Then a gusty wind came, and again my slightly open umbrella was caught in the blustery wind. We were swept off the ice just as it caved in.

I saw Kitty heading over a hill just then. The wind only carried us to the foot of the hill, and then it became very still. We were gently let down to the ground. We climbed the hill together, holding hands. I held on to the umbrella as if it was a lost friend found. I thought of this because it had so far saved us twice. My brother and I were at this time slipping and sliding up the hill in mud and ice.

When we reached the top of the hill, we saw Kitty in the distance, completely wet and looking very cold or frozen. She was in plain view as she walked toward the barn, as if she wanted to be seen or rescued and looking as exhausted as we felt.

We walked down the hill, and then we saw beads of light. We decided to proceed carefully after all our recent fright.

Then we heard voices. When we looked and leaned in close, we realized it was our parents and a search team, not an alien or a ghost! There they were, way down near the barn. The beads of light were their flashlights, and so we started to shout and scream. But then we saw our kitty run past them toward a raging cold, partly-frozen stream. So we took a few steps in the direction of the barn, but then the rain started up again. We opened the magic umbrella, and as we walked into the darkness, the wind came up and swept us away to the edge of the wooded area where Kitty was headed near the stream.

At this point, we decided that the adventure was too exciting to end on a negative note. I admit we became a little too sure that Kitty was actually going to be saved by us! When we got Kitty, we would never ever allow her out again.

Pop, pop, bang!

A tree fell and snagged my yellow coat. Then as I pulled free and began to walk, I stumbled on some rocky terrain and fell.

Uh-oh, what is that pain? Is my ankle broken?

I pulled up my pajama's leg to view my sore foot, and there was a gaping cut. I suddenly started to feel something warm and wet on my face. It was Kitty giving me a big wet lick of a kiss. I didn't see Kitty coming. It seemed eerie and out of place. Then suddenly everything went black.

I sat up, and huh? I was in bed. *Was I given medicine? Did I fall on my head? Was it all a dream?* As I climbed out of my bed, I realized that my toenails seemed awfully dirty as if I had been in mud. *How did that royal-blue umbrella, the bright yellow raincoat, and those boots get in my room on a chair?* I thought as I walked down the hall, still half-asleep.

Dawn now seemed to be crowding in. Everything was different in the morning light.

My brother Aiden was in his room, safe and sound, fast asleep. Wow! There was his yellow raincoat and red boots on the chair as well, and all you could see was his tiny form, his hair, and chin!

Mom and Dad were so fast asleep they did not hear the floor creak.

Crash! Pop! Pop! Pop!

Oh no, not that sound again! I thought how nice Mr. Wind had been. He saved my brother and me, with the help of the umbrella, from the icy trees that were falling within, so precise. Perhaps Mr. Wind wasn't so mean after all. Maybe he was howling so we could find him outside our great walls.

I also remembered the cardinal rule to never leave the house in an emergency without my parents or supervision from an adult no matter what the enterprise. I decided that ignoring the sound of the wind would be wise.

I decided to get back into my bed and pulled the covers up to my nose. I never looked outside, just down at my toes. I climbed into bed, just like I had planned.

I would love to thank my mommy this morning for the magic umbrella that was earlier practically glued to my hands!

There was Kitty rolled in a big black ball, purring. She was on my bed fast asleep as I was closing my swollen eyes. I suddenly realized that unlike Kitty I did not have nine lives!

Kitty was lying at my feet on the bed. He was sleeping, or could one eye be open? It was hard to see him with that red bow. I swear he opened one green eye and winked at me. It was then I realized Kitty thinks he is free! So that is what makes the Kitty a mystery.

CPSIA information can be obtained
at www.ICGtesting.com
Printed in the USA
BVHW021539200122
626707BV00002B/8